McGRAW•HILL
HEALTH

SENIOR AUTHORS

Susan C. Giarratano-Russell

Donna Lloyd-Kolkin

PROGRAM AUTHORS

Danny J. Ballard

Alisa Evans Debnam

Anthony Sancho

 McGraw-Hill
School Division

New York   Farmington

PROGRAM AUTHORS

Susan C. Giarratano-Russell,
MSPH, Ed.D, CHES
Health Education Specialist
University Professor and Media Consultant
Glendale, California

Donna Lloyd-Kolkin, Ph.D.
Partner
Health & Education Communication
  Consultants
New Hope, Pennsylvania

Danny J. Ballard, Ed.D
Associate Professor, Health
Texas A & M University
College of Education
College Station, Texas

Alisa Evans Debnam, MPH
Health Education Supervisor
Cumberland County Schools
Fayetteville, North Carolina

Anthony Sancho, Ph.D.
Project Director
West Ed
Equity Center
Los Alamitos, California

PROGRAM REVIEWERS

Personal Health
Josey H. Templeton, Ed.D
Associate Professor
The Citadel, Military College of South Carolina
Charleston, South Carolina

Growth and Development
Jacqueline Ellis, M Ed, CHES
Health Education Consultant
Brunswick, Maine

Emotional and Intellectual Health
Donna Breitenstein, Ed.D
Professor of Health Education
Appalachian State University
Boone, North Carolina

Family and Social Health
Betty M. Hubbard, Ed.D, CHES
Professor, Department of Health Sciences
University of Central Arkansas
Conway, Arkansas

Nutrition
Celia J. Mir, Ed.D, RD, LD, CFCS
Associate Professor, Nutrition
University of Puerto Rico
Rio Piedras, Puerto Rico

Physical Fitness
James Robinson III, Ed.D
Visiting Professor of Health
Department of Health and Kinesiology
Texas A & M University
College Station, Texas

Disease Prevention and Control
Linda Stewart Campbell, MPH
Executive Director
Minority Task Force on AIDS
New York, New York

Alcohol, Tobacco, and Drugs
Kathleen Middleton, MS, CHES
Administrator for Health and Prevention
Monterey County Office of Education
Monterey County, California

Safety, Injury, and Violence Prevention
Philip R. Fine, Ph.D, MSPH
  Director
Wendy S. Horn, MPH
  Project Coordinator
Matthew D. Rousculp, MPH
  Assistant to the Director
Injury Control Research Center
University of Alabama at Birmingham
Birmingham, Alabama

Andrea D. Tomasek, MPH
Epidemiologist, Injury Prevention Division
Alabama Department of Public Health
Montgomery, Alabama

Community and Environmental Health
**Martin Ayong Ayim, Ph.D, MPH,
  BSPH, CHES**
Assistant Professor of Health Education
Grambling State University
Grambling, Louisiana

Teacher Reviewers
Miriam Kaeser, OSF
Assistant Superintendent
Archdiocese of Cincinnati
Cincinnati, Ohio

Christine Wilson
3rd Grade Classroom Teacher
Stout Field Elementary School
M.S.D. of Wayne Township
Indianapolis, Indiana

Multicultural Reviewer
Sylvia Peña, Ed.D
Dean, Graduate Studies
University of Texas at Brownsville
Brownsville, Texas

HEALTH ADVISORY BOARD MEMBERS

Lucinda Adams
State Advisor, Health Education
Former Director of Health
Dayton City Schools District
Dayton, Ohio

Clara Arch-Webster
Vice Principal
Duval County Schools
Jacksonville, Florida

Linda Carlton
Coordinator, Elementary Science & Health
Wichita, Kansas Public Schools USD 259
Wichita, Kansas

John Clayton
6th Grade Health Teacher
Orangewood Elementary School
Phoenix, Arizona

Pam Connolly
Subject Area Coordinator/HS Teacher
Diocese of Pittsburgh
Pittsburgh, Pennsylvania

Larry Herrold
Supervisor of Health Education, K–12
Baltimore County Public Schools
Baltimore, Maryland

Hollie Hinz
District Health Coordinator and
  Health Teacher
Menomonee Falls School District
Menomonee Falls, Wisconsin

Karen Mathews
5th Grade Teacher
Guilford County School
Greensboro, North Carolina

Patty O'Rourke
Health Coordinator
Cypress-Fairbanks I.S.D.
Houston, Texas

Sarah Roberts
6th Grade Health Teacher
McKinley Magnet School
Baton Rouge, Louisiana

Lindsay Shepheard
Health & Physical Education
  Program Coordinator
Virginia Beach City Public Schools
Virginia Beach, Virginia

Bob Wandberg
Health Education Curriculum & Instruction
Bloomington Public Schools
Bloomington, Minnesota

McGraw-Hill School Division
A Division of The McGraw-Hill Companies

Copyright © 2000 McGraw-Hill School Division, a Division of the Educational and
Professional Publishing Group of The McGraw-Hill Companies, Inc.

McGraw-Hill School Division
1221 Avenue of the Americas
New York, New York 10020

Printed in the United States of America
ISBN 0-02-277367-3 / 1
  2 3 4 5 6 7 8 9 071 05 04 03 02 01 00 99

CONTENTS

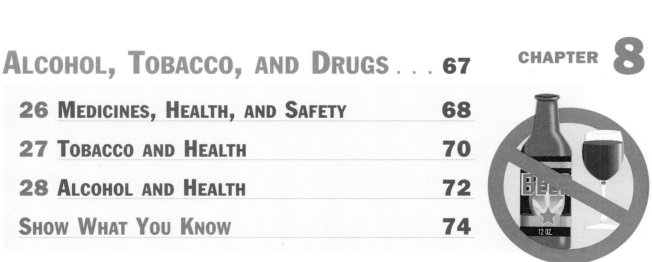

 **HANDBOOK**

McGraw-Hill Health and the Health Pyramid

McGraw-Hill Health was created to help you be as healthy as you can be. The McGraw-Hill Health Pyramid shows what you need to reach the goal of good health.

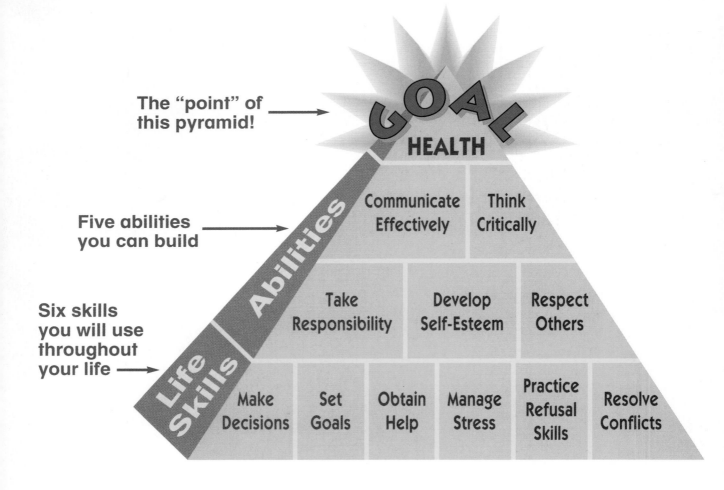

The "point" of this pyramid! →

Five abilities you can build →

Six skills you will use throughout your life →

GOAL HEALTH

Abilities

Communicate Effectively | Think Critically

Take Responsibility | Develop Self-Esteem | Respect Others

Life Skills

Make Decisions | Set Goals | Obtain Help | Manage Stress | Practice Refusal Skills | Resolve Conflicts

PERSONAL HEALTH

THE BIG IDEA

You can do many things to keep healthy.

CHAPTER CONTENTS

LESSON 1 What Is Good Health?

Good health means a healthy body.
Good health means a healthy mind.
It also means getting along with others.

HEALTHY BODY

HEALTHY MIND

GETTING ALONG WITH OTHERS

Keeping clean helps all parts of your health.
You do not become sick.
You feel good about yourself.
You get along with others.

Rest and Sleep

After a long day, your body is tired.
Rest gives your body new energy.
You need about 11 hours of sleep each night.
You may also need a nap during the day.

Getting too little sleep is unhealthy.
You may be too tired to think clearly.
You may not have the energy to play.
You may feel cranky toward people.

Healthy Teeth and Gums

Your first teeth are primary teeth.
You use them to chew, to talk—and to smile.
Your 20 primary teeth will fall out.
In their place, 32 permanent teeth will grow.

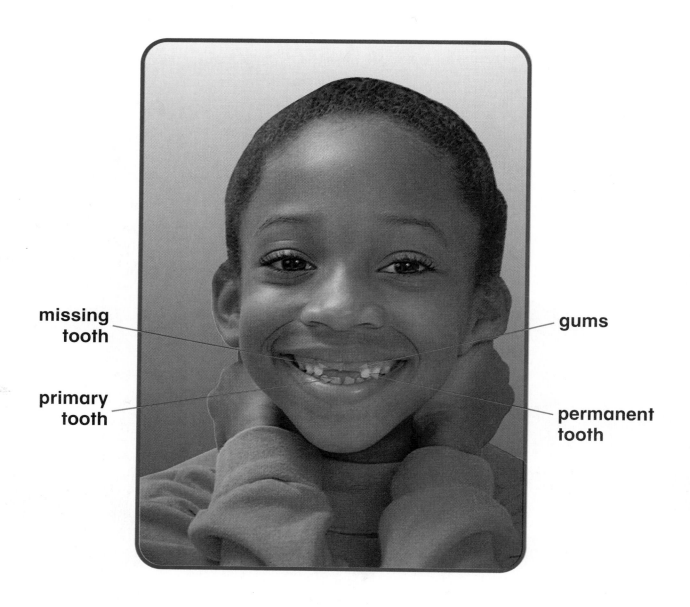

missing tooth

gums

primary tooth

permanent tooth

6

You must care for your primary teeth.
You need to brush and floss them each day.
Brushing removes food and germs.
Flossing cleans between your teeth.

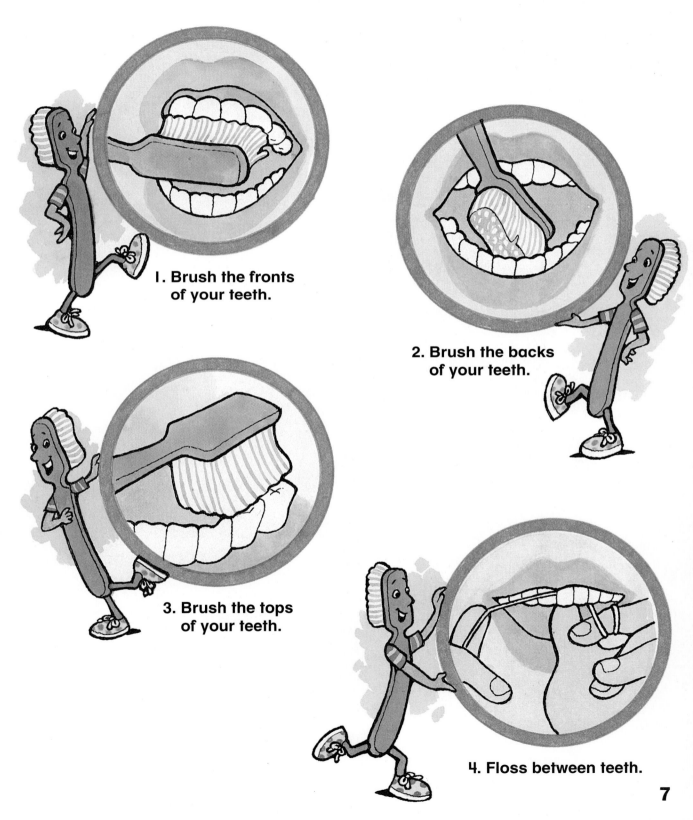

1. Brush the fronts of your teeth.

2. Brush the backs of your teeth.

3. Brush the tops of your teeth.

4. Floss between teeth.

Taking Care of Eyes, Ears, and Skin

Your senses help you learn about the world.
Name something the girl might see.
What might she hear?
What might she touch?

Your senses help you stay safe.
What can you use to keep your eyes safe?
What can you use to keep your ears safe?
What can you use to keep your skin safe?

Show What You Know

A. Write **healthy body** or **healthy mind**.

B. **3.** You want to get up at 7 tomorrow morning.
What would be a good time to go to bed?

C. Write a sentence.
Name what is shown.
Tell how you would
use it.

D. **6–7.** Write the word that
names each sense.

6.

7.

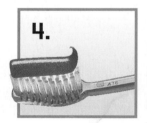 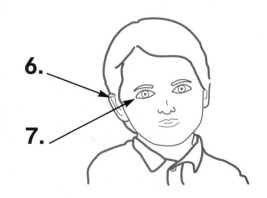

| sight | hearing | touch |

GROWTH AND DEVELOPMENT

THE BIG IDEA

Knowing how you grow
and how your body works
can help you stay healthy.

Your Body

Your body is made of many parts.
Some parts are on the outside.
Which outside body parts is this girl using?

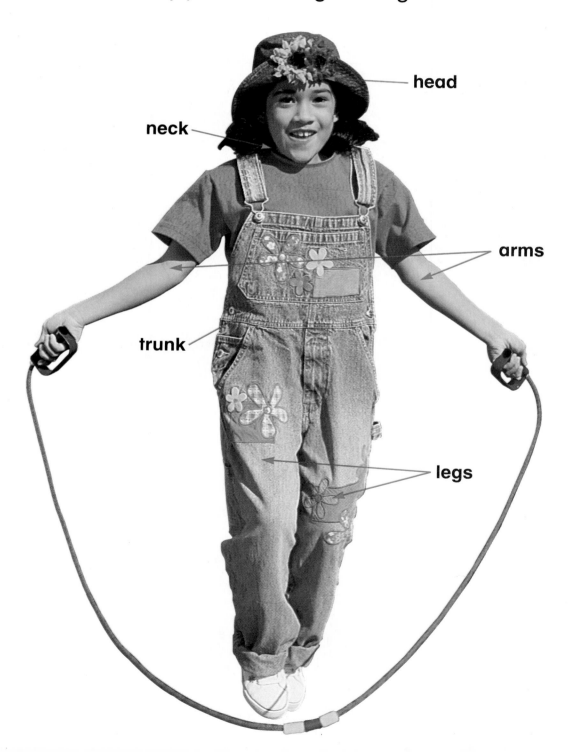

head

neck

arms

trunk

legs

Some body parts are inside the body.
Bones and muscles help you move.
What do the other inside body parts do?

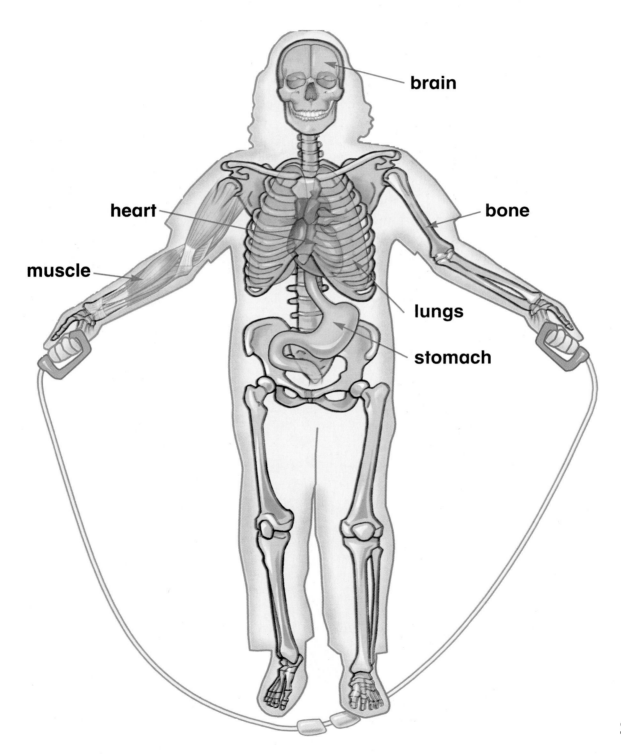

brain

heart

bone

muscle

lungs

stomach

Your senses help you learn about the world.
The girl uses her tongue to taste.
What body part helps her smell?

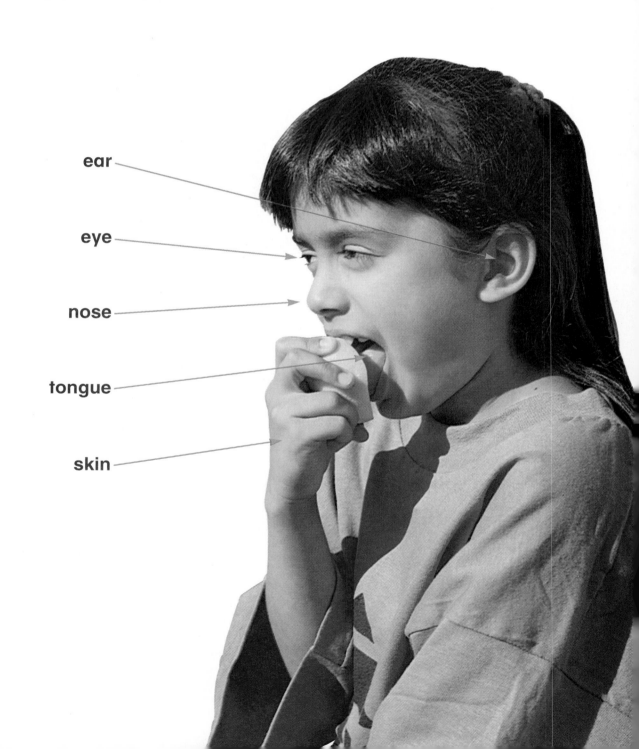

ear

eye

nose

tongue

skin

You have five senses.
They are sight, hearing, touch, smell, and taste.
Which body part goes best with each sense?

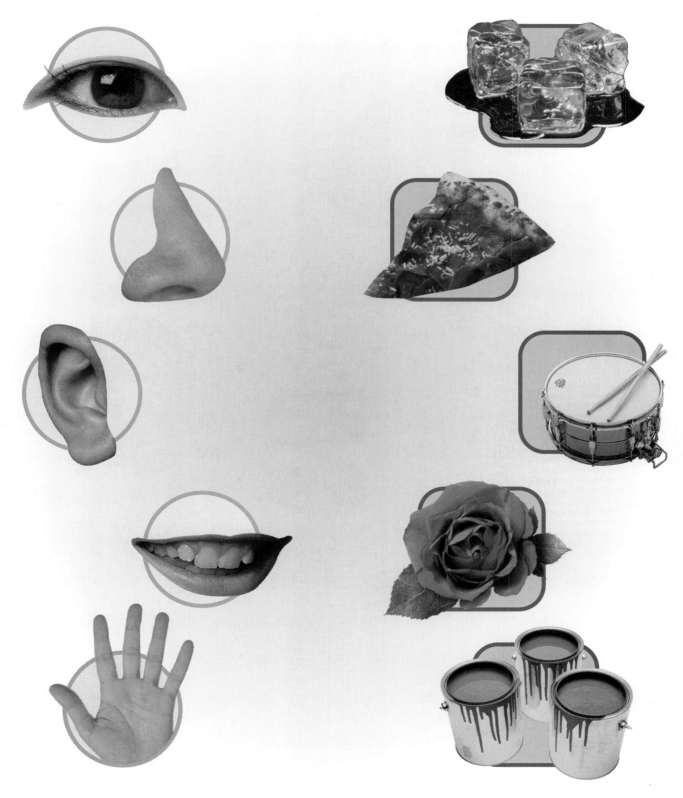

LESSON 7

Your Body Grows and Changes

Your body grows and changes.
How have these children changed?

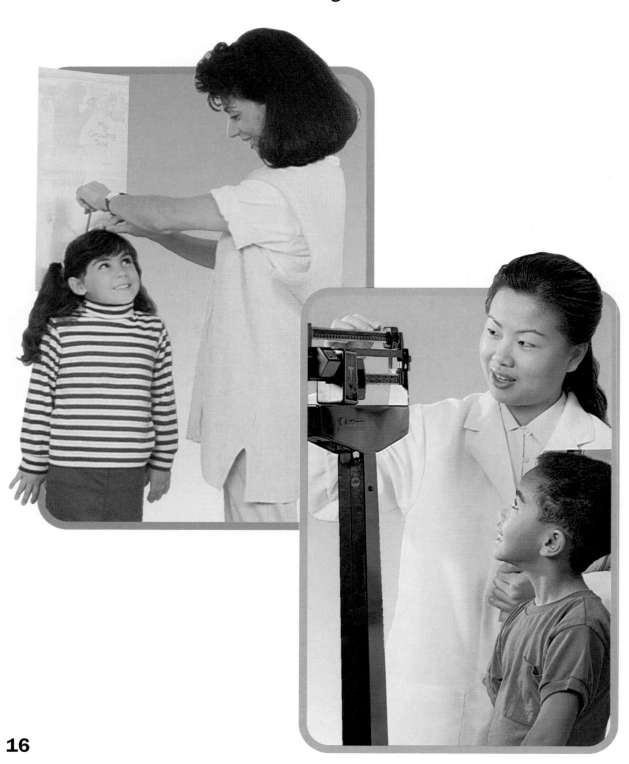

As you get older, you learn new things.
What has the older boy learned to do?
What new thing have you learned to do?

LESSON 8 — The Life Cycle

You began life as a baby.
Then you grew until you became a child.
What will you become next?

As you grow, your body changes size.
You learn new skills.
What would you like to do as an adult?

A. **1–3.** Write the word that names each body part.

> **brain** **heart**
>
> **lungs**

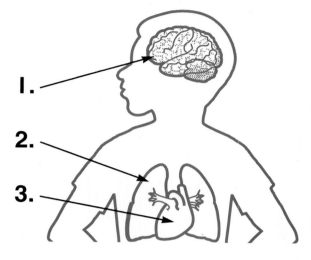

1.

2.

3.

B. **4–6.** Write the sense that goes with each body part.

> **touch** **taste** **smell**
>
> **hearing** **sight**

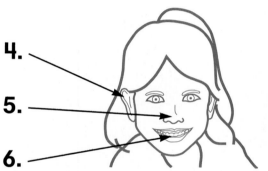

4.

5.

6.

C. **7–8.** Name two ways your body changes as it grows.

D. Name the life stage shown in each picture.

9.

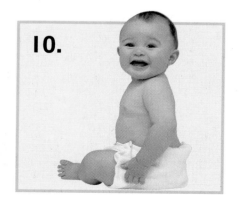

10.

EMOTIONAL AND INTELLECTUAL HEALTH

THE BIG IDEA

Healthy people feel good about themselves, get along with others, and manage stress.

CHAPTER CONTENTS

LESSON 9 — Showing Your Feelings

Everyone has feelings.
A big smile shows happiness.
Tears may show fear or sadness.
How do you think this child feels?

Healthy people share their feelings.
They talk about feeling angry or happy.
Sharing lets others know how you feel.
Sharing also helps you understand
your own feelings better.

LESSON 10 Getting Along with Others

A friend is someone that you care about.
Friends listen to each other.
They help each other when they can.

24

It takes a special person to be a friend.
Sometimes a friend may ask you to
do something unsafe.
You can say "No" and still be friends.

LESSON 11 Feeling Good About Yourself

Some people can run fast.
Some people can paint great pictures.
Everyone is special in some way.
How are you special?
What do you like about yourself?

Everyone makes mistakes.
Mistakes may make you feel upset.
They also give you a chance to learn.
Always reward yourself for trying hard.

Dealing with Stress

Going to a new school can be stressful.
You haven't met your new classmates yet.
You don't know your new teacher.
What can you do to feel better?
How can you control or manage stress?

Talking to a friend helps to manage stress.
Taking deep breaths or a walk may help.
Playing hard is another way to manage stress.
How are these children managing stress?

A. Write the word that names the feeling.

B. Write the word that completes each sentence.

3. Healthy people ____ their feelings.

4. Everyone is ____ in some way.

5. A ____ is someone you care about.

| friend | special | share |

C. Tell if each sentence is **true** or **false**.

6. Playing hard helps manage stress.

7. Fighting helps to manage stress.

8. Deep breathing helps to manage stress.

FAMILY AND SOCIAL HEALTH

THE BIG IDEA

Good health means having healthy relationships with your family, friends, and classmates.

CHAPTER CONTENTS

LESSON 13 A Healthy Family

There are many kinds of families.
Some are small. Some are large.
Some children are born to a family.
Other children may be adopted.
A family may have people of many
different ages.

Members of a healthy family love
and respect each other.
They share feelings of happiness.
They share feelings of sadness.
They show kindness and help each other.

Getting Along with Your Family

Every household needs some rules.
Rules keep family members safe and healthy.
Rules teach you how to get along with others.

There are many jobs to do at home each day.
Family members help with the household chores.
Working together gets everything done.
It makes everyone in the family feel good.

Getting Along with Your Friends

A buddy is a friend you know and like.
Like families, friendships have rules, too.
Friends respect each other's feelings.
Friends are careful with each other's things.

Friends like doing things together.
They play and work together.
They help each other when they can.

LESSON 16   A Healthy Classroom

A healthy classroom is like a healthy family.
There are rules to keep order.
Rules also keep class members safe.

Everyone in a classroom helps each other.
People care for and respect one another.
Honesty is also important in a classroom.
Everyone has something to teach and learn.

4 Show What You Know

A. Write **healthy family** or **healthy friendship**.

B. Tell if each sentence is **true** or **false**.

3. Rules keep a family and class safe.

4. Friends take care of each other's things.

5. In a healthy family, people yell.

6. Always respect your family and friends.

C. Write the word that completes each sentence.

7. Keeping ____ helps the classroom run smoothly.

8. In a healthy classroom, people ____ each other.

| order | respect | fight |

NUTRITION

THE BIG IDEA

Healthful foods help your body grow and stay strong.

LESSON 17 Food and Your Body

Your body needs healthful food.
Healthful food gives your body energy.
Healthful food makes your body strong.
It helps your body grow and stay well.

You use your mouth and teeth to chew food.
Chewed food moves down your throat easily.
Your stomach breaks down food.

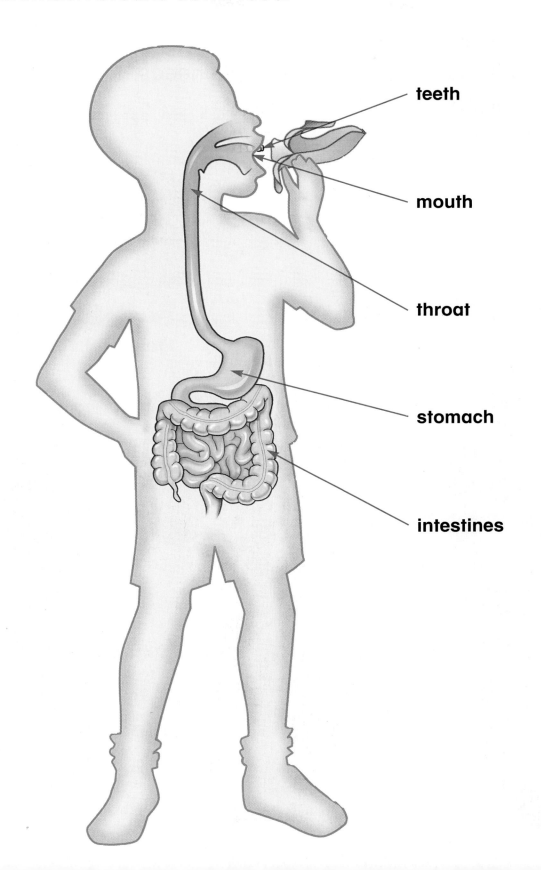

teeth

mouth

throat

stomach

intestines

Food Variety

Each food group has healthful things.
No food group gives your body all it needs.
You need food from all five groups.

Milk and Cheese Group

Meat and Fish Group

Vegetable Group

Fruit Group

Bread and Grain Group

Your body needs more food from some groups.
It needs less food from other groups.
Which groups does the body need more of?
Which groups does the body need less of?

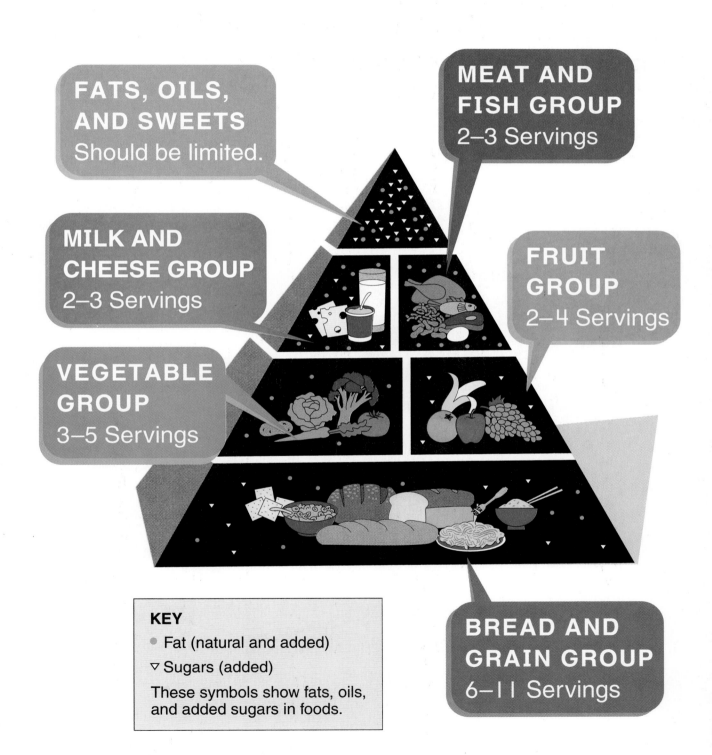

FATS, OILS, AND SWEETS
Should be limited.

MEAT AND FISH GROUP
2–3 Servings

MILK AND CHEESE GROUP
2–3 Servings

FRUIT GROUP
2–4 Servings

VEGETABLE GROUP
3–5 Servings

BREAD AND GRAIN GROUP
6–11 Servings

KEY
- Fat (natural and added)
▽ Sugars (added)

These symbols show fats, oils, and added sugars in foods.

Balanced Meals

A balanced meal has food from several groups.
Eat three balanced meals each day.
Which meal is a balanced breakfast?

Which meal is a balanced lunch?

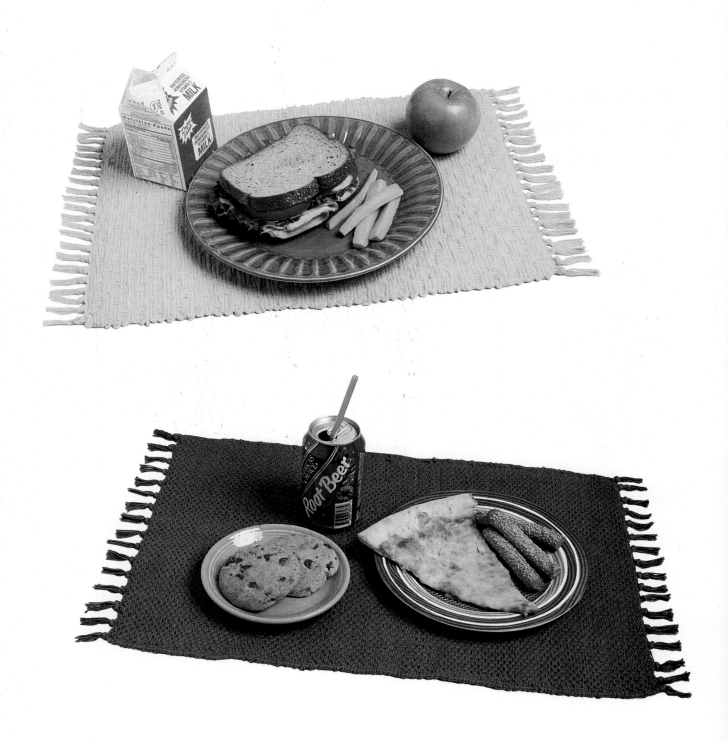

What meal do you eat each evening?
Does the food come from several groups?

LESSON 20 Healthful Snacks

Many people eat snacks between meals.
Healthful snacks give your body extra energy—
to work, to play, and to think.

Healthful snacks are low in sugar.
Healthful snacks are also low in fat and salt.
Which snacks are good for you? Why?
Which snacks are not good for you?
Why not?

A. Write the word that names each body part.

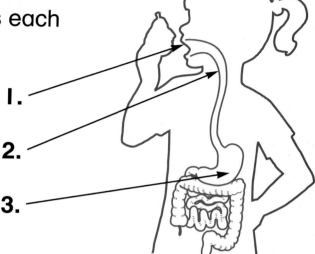

stomach

throat

mouth

1.

2.

3.

B. Write the name of the food group for each food. Would the food make a healthful snack? Explain why or why not.

4.

5.

6.

7.

8.

| bread | fruit | meat | milk | vegetable |

C. Which picture shows a balanced dinner? Explain.

9.

10.

PHYSICAL ACTIVITY AND FITNESS

THE BIG IDEA

Physical activity helps you play, work, and think better.

CHAPTER CONTENTS

Physical Activity and the Body

Bones give your body its shape. Muscles are attached to your bones and move them.

Bones and muscles help you sit, stand, and move. They help you have good posture.

Physical activity makes your body strong. Riding a bike makes your leg muscles strong. It also makes your heart and lungs strong.

The President's Challenge

The President's Challenge is a physical fitness program with five exercises. If you take part in the program, you win an award.

Presidential Physical Fitness Award

National Physical Fitness Award

Participant Award

1 Curl-ups or Sit-ups

This exercise tells how strong your stomach muscles are.

2 Shuttle Run

This exercise tells how strong your leg muscles are. It also tells how long you can run without getting tired.

3 One Mile Run/Walk

This exercise tells how strong your leg muscles are. It also tells how strong your heart and lungs are.

4 Pull-ups

This exercise tells how strong your arm and shoulder muscles are.

5 V-sit Reach

This exercise tells how easily you can bend and stretch your legs and back.

LESSON 22 Getting Fit

If you are fit, your body is strong. You can play hard without getting tired. Your body has good balance. You can bend and stretch easily.

Your body must be ready to work hard. Warm up activities get your body ready to do things.

Cool down activities slow your body down. These activities help prevent injuries and sore muscles.

Show What You Know

A. Which activity makes your muscles strong?
Which one makes your heart and lungs strong?

B. Write **good posture** or **poor posture**.

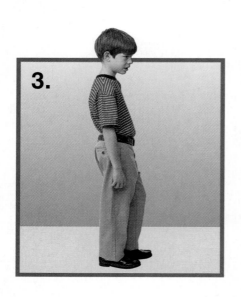

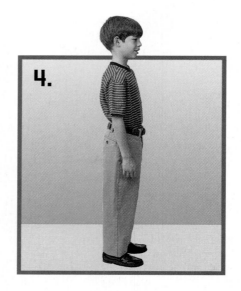

C. **5–6.** Name two reasons why you should
do warm up and cool down activities.

DISEASE PREVENTION AND CONTROL

CHAPTER 7

THE BIG IDEA

You can prevent some diseases and fight the symptoms of others.

Germs and Sickness

Everyone catches a cold once in a while. A symptom is a sign that you are ill. A fever or high body temperature is a symptom of illness. Coughs and sneezes are often symptoms of a cold.

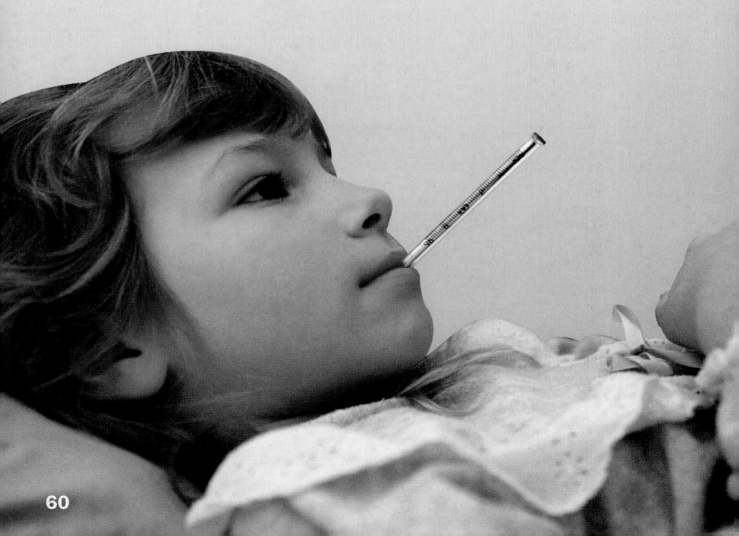

Germs cause colds, the flu, and many other illnesses. Most germs are very tiny living things. Germs are often spread in the air by sneezes and coughs.

Germs can spread from the hand to the mouth, nose, and eyes. They can also enter the body through cuts.

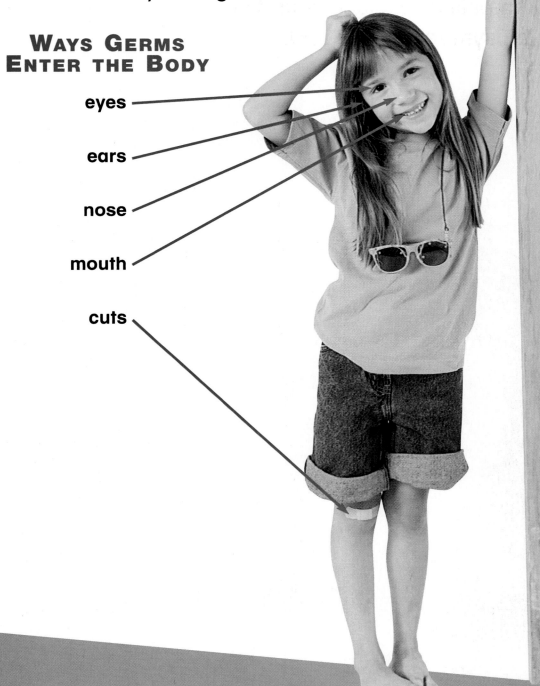

WAYS GERMS ENTER THE BODY

eyes

ears

nose

mouth

cuts

Preventing Illnesses

You can prevent germs from entering your body. Wash your hands often. Clean cuts. Cover them with a bandage. Use a tissue when you cough or sneeze.

A strong body can fight germs that enter it. What are ways to make your body strong?

STAY CLEAN

PLAY HARD

FOR A STRONG BODY

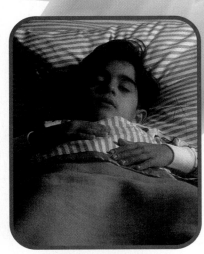

GET REST

EAT WELL

How can you get over a cold or flu quickly? You should stay home. You should get plenty of rest. You should drink lots of liquids.

When you are ill, the doctor may give you a shot. A shot has medicine to cure an illness.

During a checkup, the doctor may give you a vaccine. A vaccine is another kind of medicine. A vaccine prevents you from becoming ill.

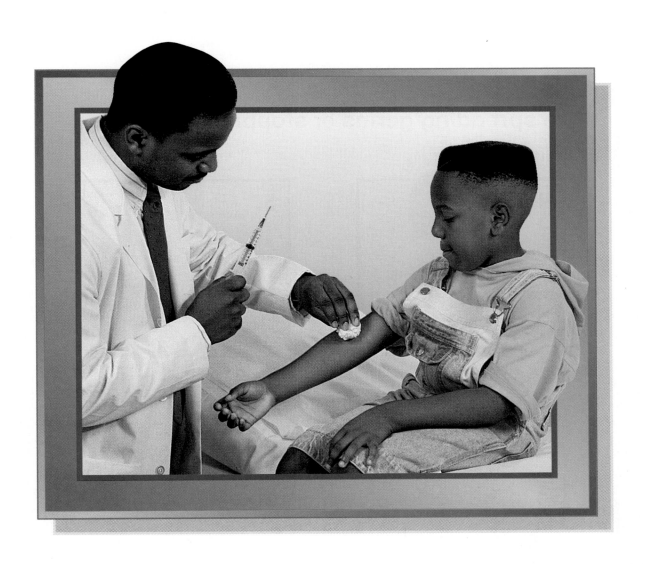

Show What You Know

A. Write the word that completes each sentence.

1. _____ are tiny things that cause illness.

2. A high body temperature means you have a _____ .

3. _____ are a symptom of a cold.

sneezes	fever	germs

B. Write **spreading germs** or **stopping germs**.

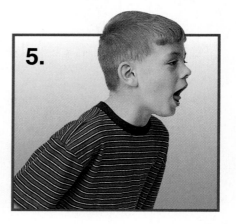

C. Write **true** or **false** about each statement.

6. A shot has medicine to cure you quickly.

7. Go to the doctor only when you feel sick.

8. A vaccine stops germs from causing illness.

ALCOHOL, TOBACCO, AND DRUGS

THE BIG IDEA

Some drugs can improve your health, but others will harm your health.

Medicines, Health, and Safety

A drug is something that can make a change in the body. A medicine is a drug that can improve health.

Some medicines kill the germs that make you ill. Others help you feel better while you are sick. A few medicines stop you from getting sick.

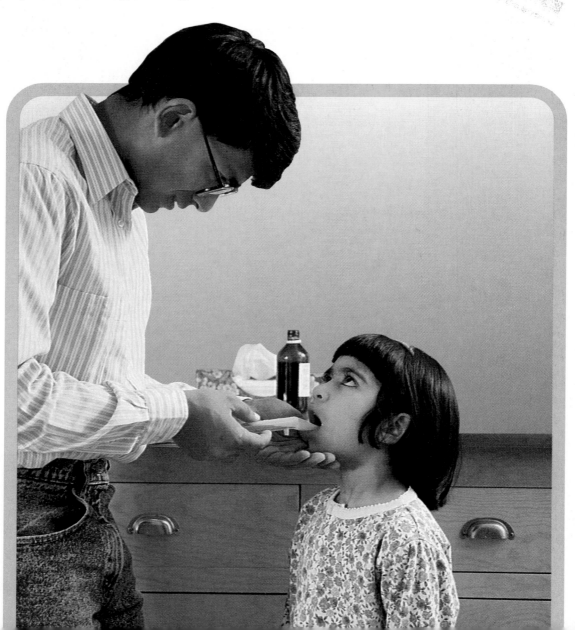

Medicines are safe only when they are used correctly. Never take medicine on your own. Take medicine only from a trusted adult.

Medicines should be stored safely at home. They should be kept away from young children.

Tobacco and Health

Tobacco is a plant. Its leaves are dried to make cigarettes and cigars. Tobacco is also made to be chewed.

Tobacco is not good for your health. Tobacco contains many things that can harm your body.

Chewing Tobacco

Using tobacco is bad for you. Your eyes may burn. Your throat may feel sore.

Using tobacco for a long time can cause serious illnesses. Some of these illnesses are cancer and heart disease.

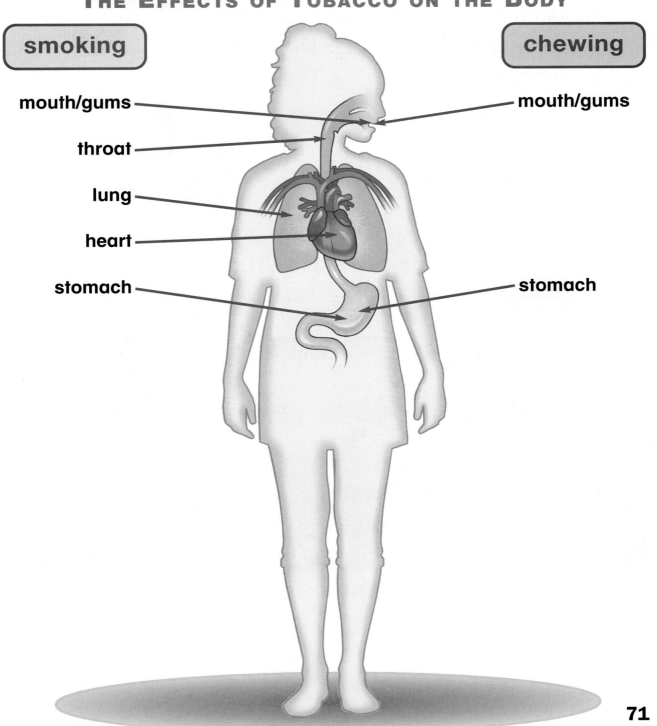

THE EFFECTS OF TOBACCO ON THE BODY

smoking | chewing

mouth/gums — | — mouth/gums

throat —

lung —

heart —

stomach — | — stomach

LESSON 28 Alcohol and Health

Alcohol is a drug found in some drinks. Alcohol is in beer and wine. Alcohol is also in liquor. Water, milk, and juice have no alcohol.

DRINKS WITH NO ALCOHOL

WATER

ORANGE JUICE

MILK

Drinking alcohol harms your health. Drinkers may feel dizzy. They may not be able to think clearly.

Alcohol can hurt many parts of your body. It can hurt your brain, throat, heart, liver, and stomach!

THE EFFECTS OF ALCOHOL ON THE BODY

Short-term effects

brain

- **fuzzy thinking**
- **slurred speech**
- **headache**
- **dizziness**

stomach

- **stomachache**

Long-term effects

hurts these body parts

brain

mouth

throat

heart

liver

stomach

8 Show What You Know

A. Write the word that names each picture.

1.

2.

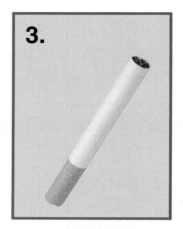

3.

| medicine | alcohol | tobacco |

B. 4–6. Name three ways medicines can help a person.

C. 7–8. Write the name of two body parts that tobacco hurts.

D. 9–10. Write the name of two body parts that alcohol hurts.

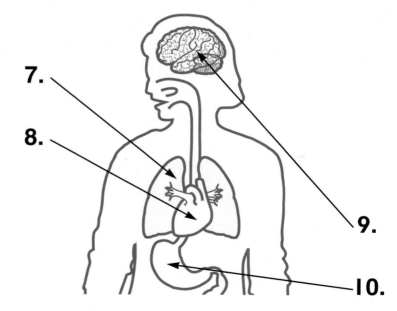

7.

8.

9.

10.

SAFETY AND INJURY PREVENTION

You can prevent most injuries by following safety rules.

CHAPTER CONTENTS

Harmful Household Substances

Many household products are hazards. They contain poisons. A poison is something that harms people.

Some products can make you sick if you eat or drink them. Glue can make you sick if you inhale, or breathe it in.

Some household products have strong poisons. Poisons can kill people. Always read the warning on a product. Never touch dangerous products. Tell an adult if you see unsafe products.

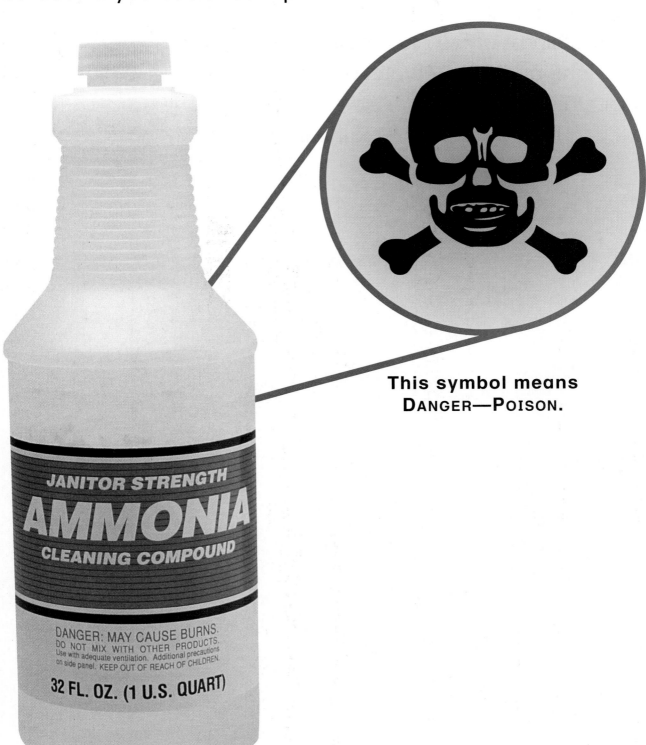

This symbol means DANGER—POISON.

JANITOR STRENGTH
AMMONIA
CLEANING COMPOUND

DANGER: MAY CAUSE BURNS.
DO NOT MIX WITH OTHER PRODUCTS.
Use with adequate ventilation. Additional precautions
on side panel. KEEP OUT OF REACH OF CHILDREN.

32 FL. OZ. (1 U.S. QUART)

Safety on the Road

Traffic rules, lights, and signs keep us safe when we walk. Always cross a street at the crosswalk. Look left, right, and then left again. Cross when the light is green or says WALK.

Drivers and bicycle riders must use signals. They must obey signs and traffic lights.

Everyone in a car should wear a seat belt. As a rider, always sit quietly. Remember to keep your hands inside the car.

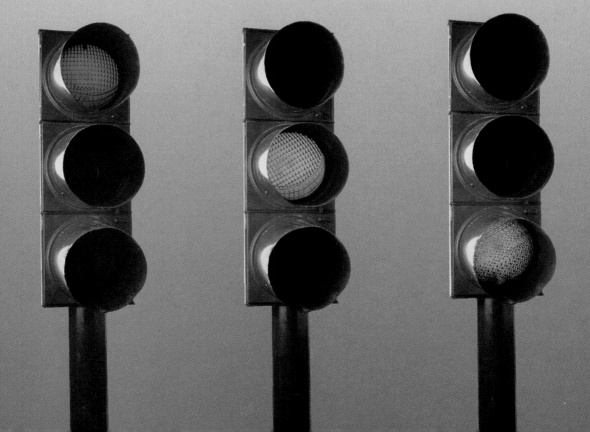

Fire Safety

A fire drill is a practice for a real fire. A fire alarm is a signal to leave the building. Follow the rules for safety during a fire drill.

FIRE DRILL RULES

1. Be quiet.
2. Line up.
3. Listen carefully.
4. Follow directions.
5. Use a fire exit.

A fire hazard can cause a fire. Matches, lighters, and stoves are fire hazards. Never touch or play with fire hazards.

If you see a fire hazard, show it to an adult. If you see a fire, tell an adult right away.

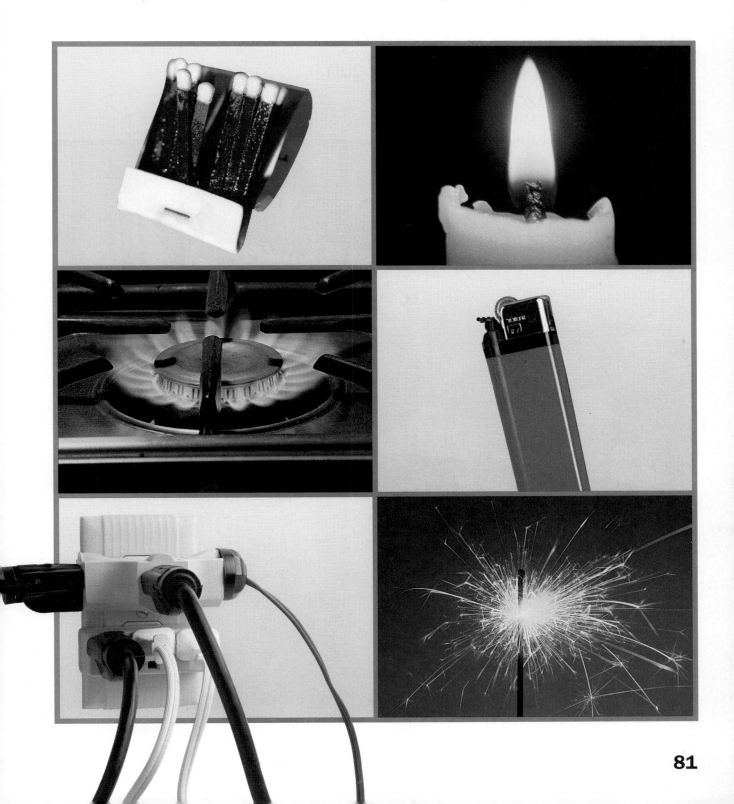

When you are home alone, keep yourself and the house safe. Follow safety rules. Always be sure to lock the door. Never touch a knife, a gun, or any other hazard.

Strangers may come to your door or phone. Never open your door to a stranger. Never tell a stranger that you are alone. Tell callers that your parent is busy. Offer to take a message.

My mother is very busy. She can't come to the phone. Do you want to leave a message?

LESSON 33 Good Touch/Bad Touch

A good touch shows caring and kindness. A handshake or a hug is a good touch. A bad touch harms you. It makes you uncomfortable. Pushing or shoving are bad touches.

Never take candy or gifts from a stranger. Never get in a car with a stranger. Always say, "No." Walk or run away. Look for and tell a trusted adult.

LESSON 34 Emergency Calls

An emergency is a dangerous situation. People may be seriously hurt and need help. Fires and car accidents are emergencies. Ambulance workers, police officers, and firefighters can help.

If you see an emergency, tell an adult. If no adult is around, go to the nearest telephone. Call 9 1 1 to tell an operator that you need help.

Tell your name, address, and phone number to the 9 1 1 operator. Describe the emergency.

My name is John Kurup. I live at 33 Dover Street.

What is the emergency?

A. Write **hazard** or **not a hazard** for each picture.

 1.

 2.

 3.

B. Write the word that completes each sentence.

4. Always cross a street at the ____.

5. A ____ traffic light means stop or don't walk.

6. Always wear a ____ when riding in a car.

> **red**   **crosswalk**   **seat belt**

C. Write **true** or **false** for each statement.

7. Pushing a person is a bad touch.

8. It's okay to get in a car with a stranger.

9. For an emergency, tell an adult or call 911.

10. When home alone, you can cook on the stove.

COMMUNITY AND ENVIRONMENTAL HEALTH

THE BIG IDEA

Everyone can help keep their environment and their community healthy.

CHAPTER CONTENTS

A community is a place where people live. It is also a place where people work and play. Some people work to keep us healthy. They are called health care workers.

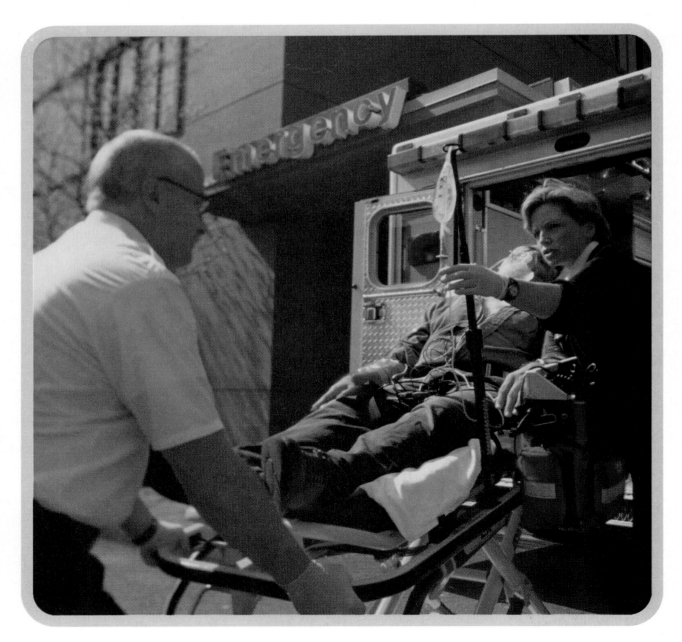

Doctors and nurses are health care workers. Some of them work at a hospital. Other doctors and nurses work in an office. Dentists are doctors who care for teeth. Pharmacists prepare medicines for people.

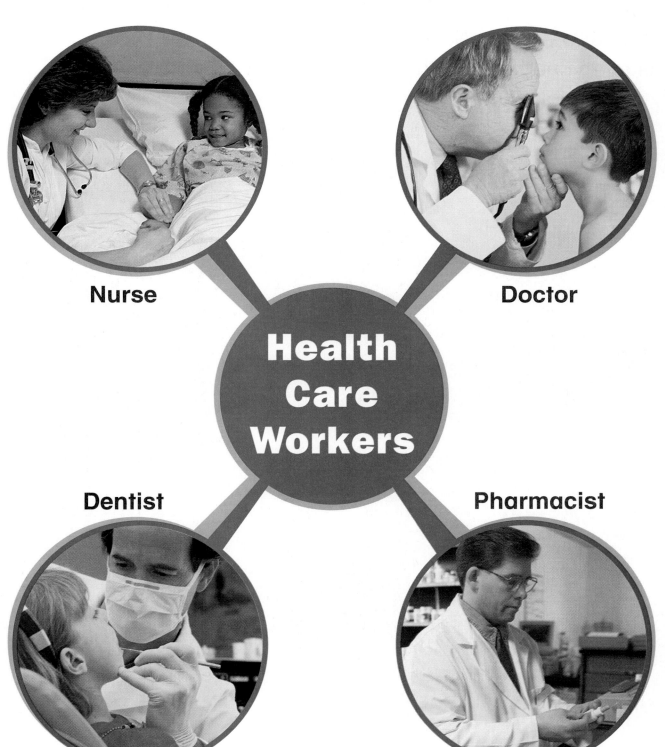

Nurse

Doctor

Health Care Workers

Dentist

Pharmacist

Pollution and Your Health

The environment is everything around you. Pollution makes the environment dirty and unhealthy. A clean environment is everyone's job.

Land

Air

Water

Noise

You can help stop pollution. You can recycle paper, glass, and cans. You can reuse something instead of throwing it away. You can reduce how much of something you use.

Recycle

Reuse

Reduce

A. Write the word that names each health care worker.

 1.

 2.

doctor	dentist	pharmacist

B. Write **air pollution** or **land pollution**.

 3.

 4.

C. Write a sentence. Tell how each person is helping to stop pollution.

 5.

 6.

Life Skill 1: Make Decisions

Part of growing up is making your own decisions. Some decisions only matter for today. What to wear to school matters only for the day.

Some decisions are important for a long time. Eating healthful foods is a life-long decision.

Here's how you can make decisions.

Life Skill 1

MAKE DECISIONS

1. See that you need to make a decision.

2. State the problem.

3. List some choices you could make.

4. Think about how each choice could come out.

5. Decide on one of the choices.

6. Make sure you made a good decision.

Life Skill 2: Set Goals

A goal is something you want to do. It is something you must work for. You might set a goal to be a good soccer player.

Here's how you can set goals.

Life Skill 2

SET GOALS

1. Choose a goal. Write it down.
2. List things needed to reach the goal.
3. List people who can help you reach the goal.
4. Set a time to reach the goal.
5. Check how you are doing.
6. When you reach the goal, reward yourself.

Life Skill 3: Obtain Help

Part of good health is knowing when you need help. You can get help from many different people. A trusted adult can help with many problems. Police or firefighters can be called in an emergency.

Here's how you can obtain help.

Life Skill 3

OBTAIN HELP

1. Know when you need help.
2. Know the difference between emergency help and another kind of help.
3. Think about who can help you.
4. Tell that person what kind of help you need.
5. Be sure the person understands what is wrong.

Life Skill 4: Manage Stress

Stress is an uncomfortable feeling. It can be caused by people, places, or things. Sometimes stress can be helpful. Too much stress is not good. You might have trouble sleeping, eating, or doing your homework.

Here's how you can manage stress.

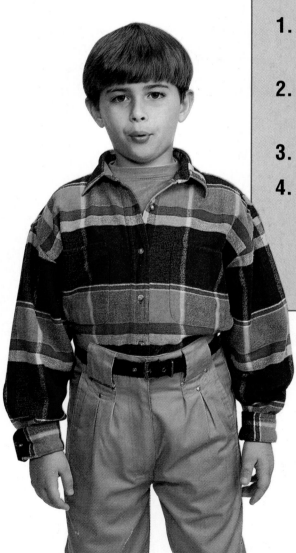

Life Skill 4

MANAGE STRESS

1. Plan how you spend your time.
2. Gets lots of rest, sleep, and physical activity.
3. Eat healthful foods.
4. Try to relax. Take deep breaths.
5. Talk with a trusted friend or adult.

Life Skill 5: Practice Refusal Skills

One way to stay healthy is to say "no."
Refusal skills help you say "no" to something
that is wrong or not healthful.

To decide when to say "no," think about
what is right for you. Ask yourself, "Is this good
for me?"

Here's how you can practice refusal skills.

Life Skill 5

PRACTICE REFUSAL SKILLS

1. Say NO right away to unsafe or unhealthful things.

2. Use a strong voice to show you mean what you say.

3. Tell why you said no.

4. Talk about better, safer choices.

5. Walk away if you need to.

Life Skill 6: Resolve Conflicts

People do not always have the same likes and dislikes. Sometimes they disagree. A strong disagreement is a conflict.

Stay away from a conflict when you can. If you can't, find a way to end it peacefully.

Here are five steps you can follow to resolve conflicts.

Life Skill 6

RESOLVE CONFLICTS

1. Accept people as they are.

2. Don't call people names. Don't make fun of them.

3. Try to understand how the other person feels.

4. Try to meet the other person halfway without doing anything unhealthful or unsafe.

5. Think about talking it over later. If you must, just walk away.

CREDITS

EDITORIAL DEVELOPMENT AND PRODUCTION:
Gramercy Book Services, Inc.

ILLUSTRATIONS: Olivia Cole-Hauptfleisch: p. 7; Barbara Cousins: pp. 13, 43, 71, 73; Rob Dunlavey: pp. 10, 69, 70, 76; Tom Sperling: pp. 54, 55.
PHOTOGRAPHY CREDITS: All photographs are by the McGraw-Hill School Division (MHSD) and Ken Karp for MHSD except as noted below.

iii: b. © PhotoDisc; v: t. © Bonnie Kamin/PhotoEdit; **Chapter 1** 2: tr. © PhotoDisc; 2: b. © PhotoDisc; 3: tl. © Gary Buss/FPG International; 3: tr. © Myrleen Ferguson/PhotoEdit; 3: b. © Tony Freeman/PhotoEdit; 5: © PhotoDisc; 6: © Myrleen Ferguson/PhotoEdit; 8: © PhotoDisc; 9: © Richard Hutchings/PhotoEdit; 10: tl. © PhotoDisc; 10: tr. © PhotoDisc; 10: bl. © C. K. Laubacher/FPG International; **Chapter 2** 14: © Michael Newman/PhotoEdit; 15: 1l. © PhotoDisc; 15: 1r. © PhotoDisc; 15: 2l. © PhotoDisc; 15: 2r. © PhotoDisc; 15: 3l. © PhotoDisc; 15: 4l. © PhotoDisc; 15: 4r. © PhotoDisc; 15: 5l. © PhotoDisc; 15: 5r. © PhotoDisc; 16: tl. © Myrleen Ferguson/PhotoEdit; 16: br.© Jim Cummins/FPG International; 17: t. © PhotoDisc; 17: b. © PhotoDisc; 18: © PhotoDisc; 20: l. © PhotoDisc; 20: r. © PhotoDisc; **Chapter 3** 23: t. © Laura Dwight/PhotoEdit; 23: b. © PhotoDisc; 24: © Tony Freeman/PhotoEdit; 26: © Nancy Richmond/The Image Works; 27: © Myrleen Ferguson/PhotoEdit; 28: © Lawrence Migdale/Stock Boston; 29: l. © Superstock; **Chapter 4** 32: tl. © PhotoDisc; 32: tr. © PhotoDisc; 32 br. © PhotoDisc; 33: © PhotoDisc; 34: t. © PhotoDisc; 34: m. © Tony Freeman/PhotoEdit; 35: b. © Richard Hutchins/PhotoEdit; 36: © PhotoDisc; 37: © PhotoDisc; 40: tl. © PhotoDisc; 40: tr. © PhotoDisc; **Chapter 5** 42: © PhotoDisc; 48: bl. © PhotoDisc; 48: br. © Frederick McKinney/FPG International; 50: t1. © PhotoDisc; 50: t2. © PhotoDisc; 50: t3. © PhotoDisc; 50: t4. © PhotoDisc; 50: t5. © PhotoDisc; 50: bl. © PhotoDisc; 50: br. © PhotoDisc; **Chapter 6** 53: © Sally Moskol/The Picture Cube, Inc.; 56: t. © Dean Abramson/Stock Boston; 56: b. © Bob Daemmrich/Stock Boston; 57: l. © Bob Daemmrich/Stock Boston; 57: r. Bonnie Kamin/PhotoEdit; 58: tl. © Bob Daemmrich/The Image Works; 58: tr. © Ariel Skelley/The Stock Market; **Chapter 7** 60: © PhotoDisc; 62: b. © Index Stock; 63: tr. © Ginny Ganong Nichols/Viesti Associates, Inc.; 64: © Bob Daemmrich/Stock Boston; 65: © Tom McCarthy/The Picture Cube, Inc.; 66: l. © James Levin/FPG International **Chapter 8** 68: © Ellen Senisi/The Image Works; 72: l. © PhotoDisc; 72: m. © PhotoDisc; 72: r. © PhotoDisc; 74: l. © PhotoDisc; 74: r. © PhotoDisc; **Chapter 9** 77: © Kathy Tarantola/The Picture Cube, Inc.; 78: © Bob Daemmrich/Stock Boston; 79: t. © Phil Borden/PhotoEdit; 79: bl. © PhotoDisc; 79: bm. © PhotoDisc; 79: br. © PhotoDisc; 81: tl. © PhotoDisc; 81: tr. © M. Antman/The Image Works; 81: ml. © Tony Freeman/PhotoEdit; 81: mr. © Chris Sorensen/The Stock Market: 81: bl. © PhotoDisc; 81: br. © Byron/The Stock Market; 83: © Jeff Dunn/The Picture Cube, Inc.; 86: © Glenn Kulbako/The Picture Cube, Inc.; 87: t. © Tony Freeman/PhotoEdit; 87: b. © John Boykin/The Picture Cube, Inc.; 88: l. © Super Stock; **Chapter 10** 90: © PhotoDisc; 91: tr. © Adam Smith/FPG International; 91: bl. © Ed Wheeler/The Stock Market; 91: br. © PhotoDisc; 92: tr. © PhotoDisc; 92: bl. © PhotoDisc; 92: br. © Robert Brenner/PhotoEdit; 94: tl. © PhotoDisc; 94: tr. © PhotoDisc; 94: ml. © PhotoDisc; 94: mr. © PhotoDisc; 94: bl. © PhotoDisc; 94: br. © PhotoDisc.